Max Finder

The Case of the Snake Escape

and Other Mysteries

To Melanie, who found Max mysteries when there were none and helped me navigate every plot twist along the way.
- Liam

This edition first published in 2011 by
Franklin Watts
338 Euston Road
London NW1 3BH

Franklin Watts Australia
Level 17/207 Kent Street
Sydney NSW 2000

Paperback original

First published in Canada by Owlkids Books Inc.

Comic colouring: Peter Dawes
Illustrations: p. 16, 22, 28, 40, 46, 64, 72, John Lightfoot
Photos: p. 52, Angela Pilas-Magee
Series design: John Lightfoot/Lightfoot Art & Design Inc.
UK edition designers: Jonathan Hair and Anna-Marie D'Cruz

A CIP catalogue record for this book is available from the British Library

ISBN: 978 1 4451 0603 8
Dewey classification: 741.5'971

Printed in China

Franklin Watts is a division of Hachette Children's Books,
an Hachette UK company.

www.hachette.co.uk

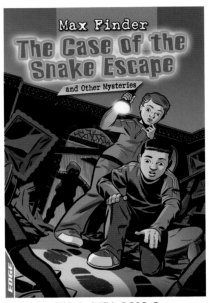

978 1 4451 0603 8

978 1 4451 0604 5

978 1 4451 0605 2

978 1 4451 0606 9

Max Finder
The Case of the Snake Escape
and Other Mysteries

Liam O'Donnell
Michael Cho

LONDON•SYDNEY

Max Finder
The Case of the Snake Escape
and Other Mysteries

Contents

Cases

Max Finder
The Case of the Snake Escape
and Other Mysteries

Contents

Puzzles

Extra Stuff

HEY MYSTERY FANS!

Welcome to the **Max Finder Mysteries**! Alison and I are really excited to bring you ten of the best mysteries to hit our town of Whispering Meadows.

From the **Basketball Card Foul** to the **White Pine Werewolf**, each mystery is crammed with clues, stuffed with suspects, and riddled with enough red herrings to keep you guessing until the last panel.

We've done all the legwork, but solving the mystery is up to you! Read the mysteries, follow the clues and try to crack the case. All the solutions are in the back of the book. But remember: real detectives never peek.

So, fire up your mystery radar and get solving!

Max

P.S. Check out the BONUS puzzles and character profiles, too!

Basketball Card Foul

Max Finder
MYSTERY

The Case of the Basketball Card Foul

Did you know a Canadian named James Naismith invented basketball in 1891? Another fact from me, Max Finder: ace detective. The boys' basketball team is playing the first game of the season. From the way Coach Sweeny is jumping around, you'd think it was the championship finals.

Time out!

METEORS

Ethan, are you okay? You seem distracted out there.

He's worn out from bragging about his precious Vince McGrady card!

After the time out, Ethan sunk a couple of baskets and the team pulled ahead. But it wasn't enough to impress Crystal Diallo.

Vince McGrady is a basketball star. Ethan Webster, the team captain, brought his limited edition McGrady rookie card to school today. It was in mint condition and he wanted to show it off.

Basketball players are total dorks! Let's get out of here.

I've had enough of Ethan and his basketball bullies, too.

Thanks to Ethan, our team won the game. But he looked too worried to celebrate.

Max Finder, someone stole Vince McGrady!

I couldn't blame Leo for leaving. When Ethan wasn't playing sports, he was picking on smaller kids like Leo.

In the fourth quarter, Josh "Rumbler" Spodek sprained his arm. Coach Sweeny helped him out of the gym and went to get some ice. Rumbler got his nickname because his voice is so deep.

Before the game, I put my Vince McGrady card in my gym bag. When I got back to the changing room, the card was gone!

Someone must have sneaked into the boys' changing room during the basketball game and taken it.

That's what you get for bragging.

Zip it, Rumbler, or you'll have more than a sprained arm to cry about!

I've got to get that card back!

Don't worry, Ethan. We'll find out who stole Vince McGrady.

We all agreed to start our investigation the next day after school.

I didn't think Rumbler would pass up a chance to visit his favourite comic shop.

He said his arm is too sore to even pick up a basketball card. His mum wants him to stay at home this weekend.

PLAYERS COMICS AND CARDS DEN

Inside the comic shop we asked about the card.

MEGA·CON MEGA COLLECTORS COMICS + CARDS SHOWCASE!

I just got off the phone with a girl who was looking to sell that card. I sent her to the comics and cards show this weekend to find a buyer.

Does that mean our thief is a girl?

Let's go to the show and find out.

The comic convention started the next day. We got there early so we wouldn't miss the thief.

Hey, Max, didn't you collect Bouncy Bears when you were little?

Don't remind me!

welcome MEGA-CON
BOUNCY BEARS
COMIC BOOK
SPORTS

There are so many people here. How are we going to figure out who took my card?

Because the thief goes to our school, basketball-brain!

There's coach Sweeny. He's a big basketball card collector.

Stay here. We'll go and talk to him.

Coach Sweeny was very happy. A little too happy, if you ask me.

What a great show and what a great day for me!

I'd better get out of here before my luck changes. See you!

Is it me or was coach Sweeny acting weird?

You want weird? There's Crystal Diallo checking out sports cards.

Crystal loves comic books but hates anything to do with sports. And that included Ethan Webster.

Crystal jumped as high as a superhero when she saw us.

I didn't know you liked basketball cards, Crystal.

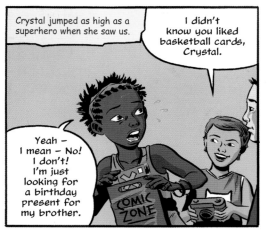

Yeah – I mean – No! I don't! I'm just looking for a birthday present for my brother.

After we said goodbye to Crystal, we spotted another surprise visitor to the card show.

There's Leo Ducharme! What is he doing here? He's not a sports fan.

And he's not a fan of Ethan. Let's go ask him a few questions.

He's running away from us!

Very strange.

When we met up with Ethan again, he was talking to one more surprise visitor to the card show.

Aren't you supposed to be at home, Rumbler?

My mum made me bring my sister to see the Bouncy Bears.

Alison and I went to discuss the case over some French fries.

The card thief is one of the people we met today, but I'm not sure which one.

Then you're buying me lunch, Mr Detective, because I know who stole Vince McGrady.

Do you know who stole the Vince McGrady basketball card? All the clues are here. Turn to page 74 for the solution.

15

Counterfeit sports cards are being sold at the Mega Collectors Comics and Cards Showcase. Help identify which one of the four cards below is fake.
What clues give it away?

45

Team: Rhinos
Position: Forward
Height: 6'7"
Weight: 212 lbs

93

Vince McGrady

YR	TEAM	GP	FG%	FT%	REB	AST	STL	BLK	PTS	AVG
04-05	Gladiators	77	.513	.758	343	182	88	28	650	8.4
05-06	Rhinos	82	.493	.743	464	246	138	48	741	9.0
TOTAL		159	.503	.751	807	428	226	76	1391	8.7

SPORTS CARDS TRADING

16

Team: Volcanoes
Position: Guard
Height: 6'9"
Weight: 230 lbs

21

Jerome Smith

YR	TEAM	GP	FG%	FT%	REB	AST	STL	BLK	PTS	AVG
04-05	Volcanoes	69	.428	.731	387	137	75	17	673	8.7
05-06	Volcaneos	75	.475	.740	405	198	71	25	728	8.9
TOTAL		156	.501	.756	600	425	124	75	1608	7.8

SPORTS CARDS TRADING

97

Team: Starfish
Position: Centre
Height: 6'3"
Weight: 180 lbs

67

Miranda Johnston

YR	TEAM	GP	FG%	FT%	REB	AST	STL	BLK	PTS	AVG
04-05	Starfish	53	.417	.702	190	96	65	19	504	7.3
05-06	Starfish	55	.433	.726	210	132	81	24	537	7.9
TOTAL		108	.425	.714	400	228	146	43	1041	7.6

SPORTS CARDS TRADING

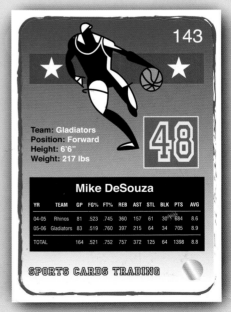

143

Team: Gladiators
Position: Forward
Height: 6'6"
Weight: 217 lbs

48

Mike DeSouza

YR	TEAM	GP	FG%	FT%	REB	AST	STL	BLK	PTS	AVG
04-05	Rhinos	81	.523	.745	360	157	61	30	684	8.6
05-06	Gladiators	83	.519	.760	397	215	64	34	705	8.9
TOTAL		164	.521	.752	757	372	125	64	1398	8.8

SPORTS CARDS TRADING

ANSWER ON PAGE 82

Midnight Scratcher

Max Finder
MYSTERY

The Case of the
Midnight Scratcher

Did you know that the first jack-o'-lanterns were carved from potatoes? Max Finder here, fact collector and ace detective. It was another lazy October Sunday here in Whispering Meadows when Alison showed up with her new friend Gabrielle Séguin and a new mystery.

Put away your wheels, Max. We've got another case.

Gabrielle just started at Central Meadows school in September and already had lots of friends.

NO FLYERS, PLEASE!

Last night, we were at Leslie Chang's birthday sleepover. While we were asleep, somebody damaged Leslie's new Avril Elliot CD. All the girls are blaming Gabrielle.

Gabrielle and Leslie had become good friends. They liked the same music and loved playing hula hoops. Gabrielle had no reason to damage Leslie's CD.

Now nobody will speak to me! I wish I never moved from Bristol.

Sounds like a set-up. Start from the beginning and tell me what happened.

It started out as a great birthday party. All Leslie's friends were there: Nanda Kanwar, Dorothy Pafko, Alison and me. We hung out, munched on snacks, and watched TV. It was fun.

When we cut the cake, Leslie's little sister Emma, her older brother Doug and her father joined us. Emma can be a pain, but the little snoop was on her best behaviour. Doug just snatched a piece of cake and hobbled back to his room on his broken ankle.

Then we opened the presents. Leslie's dad gave her the new Avril Elliot CD. It just came out and none of us had it yet. I think Nanda was jealous. She loves being the first to have the coolest music.

Avril Elliot

Big deal. I'm buying one tomorrow.

We listened to the new CD all night. When Leslie saw the disc the next morning, the party was over. Somebody had scratched my initials into the CD so it wouldn't play any more. I told them I didn't do it, but Dorothy cut me off.

Don't lie, Gabrielle. I saw you do it!

G5 RULES!

Dorothy woke in the night and said she saw me in the kitchen, hiding behind the fridge door while I scratched the CD!

I told them that no one would scratch their own initials into a CD, but they wouldn't listen. We have to find the real Midnight Scratcher, Max.

19

Gabrielle went home, and Alison and I checked out the scene of the crime: Leslie Chang's house. When we arrived, Leslie was teaching Emma a new hula hoop trick. It wasn't going well.

You'll never get it. I give up. I'm going inside.

I'm sorry if I'm not as good as Gabrielle. Give me another chance!

Leslie was happy to be rescued from her sister. She showed us the living room where they all slept during the birthday party.

That door leads to Doug's and Emma's bedrooms. I left the CD over by the stereo.

Dorothy saw Gabrielle in here during the night. She recognised the coloured toes on Gabrielle's socks.

The knife belonged to Leslie's older brother, Doug. He claimed it went missing a few days ago but didn't know how it got into the kitchen. When we asked him about the damaged CD, he just smiled.

I was asleep in my room all night. At least I won't have to hear that terrible music any more!

I think I've found our CD-scratching tool.

As we left, we found Emma practising with her hula hoop. She said she was asleep in her room during the sleepover. Before I could ask her any more questions, she ran into the house looking for her sister.

Leslie! Time to teach me more hoop tricks! You promised!

Our next step was to track down our one eyewitness: Dorothy. Back in Year 5, Leslie teased Dorothy a lot. They only became friends recently. The science whiz could still be holding a grudge against Leslie. I had to hear her story.

It was pretty dark, and I wasn't wearing my glasses, but I know I saw Gabrielle behind the fridge door.

The light from the fridge woke me up. I couldn't see Gabrielle's head, but I could tell it was her because of those coloured socks. I thought she was just getting a drink of water, so I went back to sleep.

There was one last party-goer to talk to: Nanda Kanwar. When we met up with her, Nanda was busy listening to her brand-new Avril Elliot CD.

Avril Elliot

Tell Leslie she can borrow my CD if she likes. It's totally cool!

When I finally got her to turn down the volume, I asked Nanda about Leslie's birthday party.

I didn't see anything. But I did hear somebody opening that stupid door leading to the bedrooms. It took me forever to get back to sleep!

I just can't work out who is setting you up, Gabrielle.

Great, I just moved to this town and already I have no friends.

Don't throw away your toe socks yet, Gabrielle. I know who scratched the CD and why they did it.

Do you know who the Midnight Scratcher is? Turn to page 74 for the solution. If you're stuck, try the puzzle on page 22.

CRIME SCENE TEAM

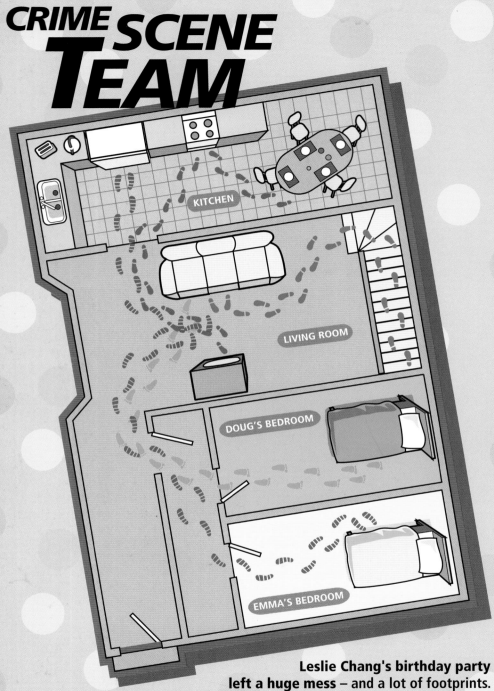

**Leslie Chang's birthday party
left a huge mess** – and a lot of footprints.
If Leslie's father had not cleaned up, Max and Alison might have had
an easier time solving this case. **You'll need to use the footprints
and the clues from the case to prove who scratched the CD.**

ANSWER ON PAGE 82

Stereo-Smashing Spook

Max Finder
MYSTERY

The Case of the Stereo-Smashing Spook

Did you know people have been celebrating Halloween for more than 3,000 years? Max Finder here, fact collector and ace detective. Tonight I'm history's greatest sleuth, Sherlock Holmes. Alison is my Scooby Doo sidekick, Velma. If you haven't guessed already, we're at our school's Halloween dance.

Max, they're going to announce the winner of the best costume. First prize is that new stereo.

This year's winner is...

Tony DeMatteo!

I knew it!

It's not fair!

Tony is a total cheat!

Everyone was mad at Tony. His dad donated the prize from his electronics store. Tony wasn't even supposed to enter. Leslie Chang had organised the dance. She tried to get Tony to return the stereo.

Give back the stereo or you'll regret ever winning it!

Forget it, Leslie. I won fair and square. It's mine and I'm keeping it!

Everyone started dancing and I thought the stereo was forgotten. But a crash from the stairwell told me I was wrong.

CRASH!

Alison, what was that?

Tony's stereo! It's ruined.

I didn't do it! Honest.

I think the culprit was trying to hide the stereo near the ticket table and the trolley rolled down the stairs.

My stereo!

Don't worry, Tony. We'll catch whoever did this.

Don't look at me. I was coming out of the toilets when I heard the crash.

Leo said someone burst out of the stairwell and ran down the hall. The person wore a black cloak, a wizard's hat and had large green feet.

Leo looked pretty scared, and my mystery radar told me he wasn't hiding anything. I couldn't say the same for the dark stairs at the end of the hall.

AAAGGHH!

The others tidied up the stereo while we investigated.

Hel . . . Hello?

RAAARR!

AAAGGHH!!

It wasn't a monster, but it was close. Basher McGintley was the biggest bully in the world and he made a perfect orc, even without the scary mask.

You jumped twice as high as Leslie Chang did!

Crawl back to Mordor, Basher.

Leslie just came through here?

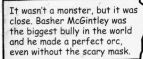

Basher said that someone in a black cloak and hat ran through the stairwell just before we did. He didn't see her face, but recognised Leslie's wizard outfit. His story matched Leo's, but something about Basher made me suspicious.

Nobody knows I'm down here, so don't tell! You'll ruin my Halloween surprise.

Nice feet, Basher. They suit your costume.

And our investigation.

Basher didn't admit to knowing about the smashed stereo, but orcs and bullies have one thing in common: they rarely tell the truth. On our way back to the dance, we stumbled on a black costume in the stairwell.

Looks like face paint.

Back at the dance, word had spread about the wrecked stereo, and Leslie Chang seemed surprised to see her cloak.

How did your hat and cloak end up in the stairwell, Leslie?

You tell me! I left them on a chair to go and dance. When I came back they were gone!

Have you seen Basher? It's his turn to help.

Leslie was surprised to hear that Basher was in the stairwell. She stormed off to find him. Dorothy Pafko shed more light on Leslie's dance-floor alibi.

I was dancing with Leslie, but she didn't dance for long. She disappeared just before the stereo was smashed.

Nanda Kanwar came running up, looking excited enough to pop a zombie zit. She had looked all over for us and had a vital piece of evidence for our investigation.

Just before the stereo was smashed, I saw Leslie in her hat and cloak wheeling the trolley out of the gym.

Hey, I saw that too! I couldn't see Leslie's face under that hat, but I laughed because she kept tripping over her big green feet.

Alison and I headed over to get a drink. This case had made us thirsty, but our ears were still working fine.

I don't think it was Leslie. I think it was Basher.

Yeah, that's why he's hiding under the stairs!

I'm ready to give up the ghost on this case. What do you think, Sherlock?

It's elementary, my dear Alison. Elementary.

Do you know who the stereo smasher is? All the clues are here. Turn to page 75 to solve the case.

Message Mix-up

Leslie Chang and Crystal Diallo accidentally ended up wearing
the same costume to the Halloween dance.
**Put the following instant messages back in order to work out what
costumes they were planning to wear and how the mix-up happened.
Write your answers on a separate piece of paper.**

File   Edit   View   Help

Talk   Invite   Block

a ☐ **Nanda says:**
Who knows? Crystal was in a rush. I gotta go too, ASAP.
Can't wait for the Halloween dance.

b ☐ **Leslie says:**
Maybe a witch. What are you going as, Nanda?

c ☐ **Crystal says:**
Don't know yet. Do you know, Leslie? My mum and I are going
shopping for it in 15 minutes. BRB

d ☐ **Nanda says:**
Frankenstein. Can't think of anything else.

e ☐ **Leslie says:**
Bye Nanda, see you at school tomorrow.

f ☐ **Crystal says:**
Great costume, Leslie! I'm sure you'll look really scary with
your green face. Okay guys, I gotta go.

g ☐ **Leslie says:**
Shouldn't take long to dress up as that green monster LOL!

h ☐ **Nanda says:**
What are you guys wearing to the Halloween dance?

i ☐ **Leslie says:**
What was that all about? I'm not painting my face to be a witch.

ANSWER ON PAGE 82

Soapy Switch

Max Finder
M Y S T E R Y

The Case of the
Soapy Switch

Did you know that a beaver can hold its breath for 45 minutes? Max Finder here, fact collector and ace detective. It's a chilly Saturday in Whispering Meadows, but it looks like a new mystery is going to heat things up.

Here comes Nanda Kanwar and she looks mad.

Max! Alison! Someone soaped my chocolate!

For the past month, every kid at our school has been selling chocolate bars to raise money for charity. Whoever sells the most wins a new snowboard. The contest closes in two days and Nanda Kanwar had a strong lead until somebody switched her chocolate bars for soap bars.

If I don't get those chocolate bars back, I won't win the snowboard!

Don't worry, Nanda, we'll catch the soap switcher.

Tell us what happened. Start from when you got the chocolate.

SNIFF!

SUDS SCENTS

Yesterday after school, I picked up my last box of chocolate bars, and went to a rehearsal for the school play. I put my jacket and the chocolates against the wall. The only other people there were Alison's brother Marcus Santos, Tony DeMatteo, the director Mrs Janssen, Sasha Price and Alex Rodriguez.

Alex and I have big parts and were on stage for the whole rehearsal. Alex is nice, and good at everything. He sold the most chocolate last year and is behind me by a few bars this year.

That's it Nanda, turn your back on Alex as you say your line.

Tony isn't interested in anything but sports. I think his mum made him audition for the school play. He plays a servant and doesn't have any lines, so he doesn't bother to make notes in his script. He hasn't sold any chocolate bars either.

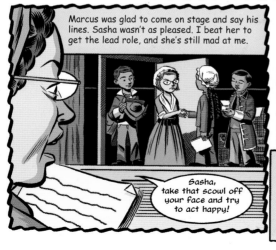

Marcus was glad to come on stage and say his lines. Sasha wasn't as pleased. I beat her to get the lead role, and she's still mad at me.

Sasha, take that scowl off your face and try to act happy!

When the rehearsal ended, Alex, Tony and I caught the late bus home. Tony sat at the back. I was tired, but Alex really wanted to practise our lines all the way home. Tony must have been full of energy because the bus driver had to tell him to sit down several times.

I went home after school and stayed in all night. This morning, I woke up and my chocolate bars were gone!

Whoever did the switch wanted you out of the running so they could win the snowboard.

We didn't have a crime scene to investigate, but we had plenty of suspects. We started close to home: Alison's house. Her brother Marcus had sold lots of chocolate and had talked about wanting to win the snowboard.

Last night, I saw Marcus come home with an extra box of chocolates!

When we tracked down Marcus, he was getting ready to sell more chocolate bars, but he didn't have the charity spirit.

I got that extra box from the school. I need it to beat Nanda and Alex and win that snowboard.

Alex was outside the Big Mart supermarket selling lots of chocolate bars. With Nanda out of the competition, Alex was probably going to win again. Despite this, he seemed pretty upset when we told him about Nanda.

chocolate FOR charity

I'm not in this for the snowboard. I just want to raise the most money for charity.

The bars of soap came from a fancy soap shop in town. We checked it out, and the owner seemed surprised when we showed her the bar I took from Nanda's box of chocolates.

BATH BOMBS VANILLA COCONUT

PEACH SOAP   FRUIT SOAP   NUT SOAP

SUDS N SCENTS

CHOC SOAP

MASSAGE BAR

ALMOND OIL BAR

Where did you get that soap? I don't sell that kind any more. It gave people a rash. I have a pile of them in the storeroom.

We were on our way out when Sasha and her mother came in. They must have been regular customers because the owner knew them by name. Sasha just smiled when we told her about Nanda.

Tell Nanda she can always buy my old snowboard! I bought a brand-new one last week.

There was one last suspect to talk to: Tony DeMatteo. He hadn't sold many chocolate bars and didn't have a chance of winning the snowboard. But he might have seen something at the rehearsal.

Buzz off, fact boy. I'm sick of hearing about chocolate bars and play rehearsals!

Solving a mystery is like building a jigsaw puzzle. This time it felt like we didn't have all the pieces. That's when Nanda arrived with a tattered script from her play, giving us another piece of the puzzle.

I accidentally picked up somebody else's script after rehearsal. It has no name or notes written in it, but look at the back page.

STEAL NANDA'S CHOCOLATE and THE SNOWBOARD IS YOURS.

There is no signature, so I guess we'll never know who stole my chocolates.

Don't give up yet, Nanda. I know who stole your chocolates.

And I know who wrote that note.

Do you know who switched the chocolate? All the clues are there. Turn to page 76 to find out.

33

Locker Stalker

Test your detective memory! Study Tony DeMatteo's messy locker for two minutes. Then, turn to page 84 and answer the questions to see what you remember.

ANSWER ON PAGE 82

Max Finder
MYSTERY

The Case of the
Sandy Ski Hill

Did you know snowflakes are smallest in really cold weather? Max Finder here, fact collector and ace detective. The holiday break is finally here, and Alison and I were shredding it up at Whispering Mountain Ski Club when Nate Yamada stopped us.

SKI PATROL

Sorry, guys. The rest of this run is closed. Something is mucking up the snow back there.

It looks like road sand. If skiers run into this, they could get hurt.

My mystery radar was beeping. I think Nate had heard about our mystery-solving hobby, because he quickly tried to shut down the investigation.

Put away your detective gear, Alison. Leave it to the ski patrol. We'll catch the person who did this. Just go and have fun.

I didn't know Nate was a ski patroller.

Yeah, I heard he got turned down for the job.

A little while later, we saw Nanda Kanwar sitting in the snow on a large patch of dirty sand. The sand dumper had struck again, but this time there was a witness.

I saw the whole thing! Somebody wearing a red and blue ski jacket dumped all this sand from a big bag and ran into the woods.

When we got to the woods, we found sand patches and some footprints in the snow.

Whoever made these was wearing ski boots.

So the sand dumper is a skier, not a boarder.

There was another set of footprints in the snow. They were made by normal winter boots, and we followed them out of the woods and into a bird lover's paradise.

This is Mr Zilkowsky's backyard! I used to come here with my grandfather. Mr Zilkowsky was always complaining about the noise from the ski club.

I heard he even went to the mayor to get the ski club closed.

He does a good job of keeping snow off his path.

CRACK!

What was that?!

Someone was skulking through the trees. Was it the sand dumper? We moved quietly through the snow to get a better look.

It's Basher McGintley and his gang. They're throwing snowballs at skiers.

Let's have a closer look.

Big mistake! It's hard to sneak up on people with a snowboard stuck to your feet. Basher and his gang heard us coming and used us for target practice.

Go play detective somewhere else!

Basher is on our suspect list for sure!

37

Basher's gang scattered when we ran into Carla Baxter. She's a ski patroller. Last week, she banned Basher and his buddies from the hill for skiing dangerously. They've been causing trouble ever since.

Nate Yamada, the chairlift operator, saw Basher take sand from the sand bins this morning and chased him away.

SKI PATROL

Carla already knew about the sand patches on the hill. She became suspicious when we told her about Nanda's fall. Carla told us that Nanda was dropped from the ski racing team for missing practice.

Nanda is probably dumping sand on the hills to get back at the ski club.

It's our job to keep the hills safe. If someone gets hurt, all the ski patrollers will be in trouble.

SKI PATROL

We've also got a thief on the hill. One of our ski patrol vests is missing! Keep your eyes open.

SKI PATROL
CARLA BAXTER

I don't trust Carla. This morning, she was on the chairlift in front of me. She was sitting with Nanda and they were arguing. Carla was really mad about something.

Mad enough to dump sand on the hills and blame Nanda?

We went to check out the sand bin at the side of the entrance road. The bin holds the sand that is spread on the road to give cars grip on the ice. On our way, we ran into Nate Yamada again. He was in a hurry.

Some old guy is stealing sand from the bin! I'm going to report him.

When we got to the bin...

That's Mr Zilkowsky!

He's stealing the sand!

EEEEP!

Mr Zilkowsky was stuffing sand into his bag like a robber grabbing cash from the till. When he saw us, he ran back into the woods, carrying his bag of stolen sand.

Beside the sand bin, we found another bag half-buried in the snow.

This backpack is half-full of sand.

That's because it belongs to the sand dumper!

Hey, Mr Detective, does that mean Mr Zilkowsky is the one?

I'll tell you at the chalet over a hot chocolate. It's your turn to buy!

Do you know who the sand dumper is? All the clues are here. Turn to page 76 for the solution.

SPY QUIZ

Test your spy skills with the true or false questions below.
Write your answers on a separate piece of paper.

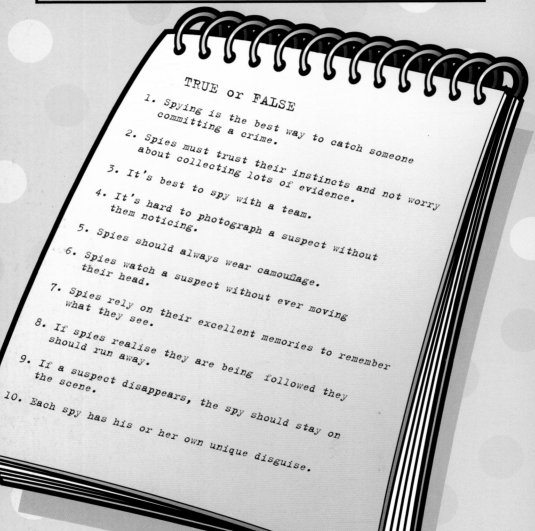

TRUE or FALSE

1. Spying is the best way to catch someone committing a crime.

2. Spies must trust their instincts and not worry about collecting lots of evidence.

3. It's best to spy with a team.

4. It's hard to photograph a suspect without them noticing.

5. Spies should always wear camouflage.

6. Spies watch a suspect without ever moving their head.

7. Spies rely on their excellent memories to remember what they see.

8. If spies realise they are being followed they should run away.

9. If a suspect disappears, the spy should stay on the scene.

10. Each spy has his or her own unique disguise.

ANSWERS ON PAGE 83

Missing Movie

NAME: DOGTOWN MALONE

REEL #2

Max Finder

MYSTERY

The Case of the Missing Movie

Did you know that people have been eating popcorn for over five thousand years? Max Finder here, fact collector and ace detective. It's Spring half-term and kids from all over town have come to the Meadows Movie Club.

THIS WEEK'S WINNER!

DOGTOWN MALONE

FINDING TUTU

No surprise *Dogtown Malone* beat *Finding Tutu* in this week's movie club vote.

Fantastic! I'll take bloodthirsty zombies over a cartoon poodle any day.

We were in the queue to get movie munchies when the popcorn machine started shooting out popcorn like a *Dogtown Malone* explosion. Trina, the manager of the cinema, raced over to fix the crazy machine.

POPCORN

EMPLOYEES ONLY

The door came off. Trina, help!

POPCORN

KLINK!

Someone loosened the screws on the door.

Trina was pretty angry that someone had sabotaged the popcorn maker. A few minutes later, she pulled us aside but was more worried than angry.

Someone stole half of the reels for *Dogtown Malone!*

Trina was taking the reels to the projectionist's booth when the popcorn maker went crazy. She put the film cans on the counter, but when she turned around, one of the cans was gone.

We can't show the movie without those missing reels. If we don't find them, I'll lose my job.

And we'll be stuck watching a totally lame poodle!

No one can find out about the missing reels! The kids will go mad if they hear we're not showing *Dogtown*.

So, we have to solve a crime without letting anyone know what we're doing?

I like that challenge. We'll take the case!

I had no idea how we were going to find the stolen movie reels without letting anyone else know they were missing. But if it gave us a chance of NOT seeing *Finding Tutu*, then I was all for it.

The thief stole the movie reels while Trina was fixing the popcorn maker. But where are they now?

EMPLOYEES ONLY

They must be close. Let's check in here.

Inside Trina's office, we talked to Alex Rodriguez, head of the movie club. Alex counts the votes and hands out door prizes. He said he was in the office alone when the popcorn maker went crazy. He didn't sound happy about the vote.

I'm sick of *Dogtown*. I was hoping *Tutu* would win. That dog is so funny!

Alex left the office to get the prizes ready. We gave the office a quick search, but didn't find any clues.

Alex doesn't like *Dogtown Malone* and he could be lying about being in here when the movie reels were taken.

Would he sabotage his own movie club just to see that dumb poodle?

Inside the cinema, we started asking kids where they were when the popcorn maker went crazy. Melanie Reece claimed to have been in her seat the whole time, but my mystery radar told me she was hiding something.

Mrs Doyle told me about the popcorn maker. She ran in here and looked scared. Then she went to the front.

Mrs Doyle said she was in Trina's office emptying the rubbish bin when the popcorn explosion happened. When she saw the flying kernels, she was startled and ran inside. She talked to Melanie and then finished picking up the rubbish.

Melanie and I don't want to see that *Dogtown* movie. Those movies are too loud and too scary for kids! I told Trina, but she wouldn't listen.

Time was running out. The seats were filling with kids expecting to see *Dogtown Malone*. If we didn't get a break in this case, the only dog they were going to get was a pink poodle.

Hey, super-sleuth. You have something stuck to your shoe.

NAME: DOGTOWN MALONE
REEL #2

It's the label from the missing movie reel. The thief brought the movie reels down here.

And I bet I know where the reels were taken.

EXIT

Movie Mad Lib

Make movie history! On a piece of paper, complete the **missing text** between the brackets in this *Dogtown Malone* movie script and then read it aloud.

Scene 4:

Dogtown Malone arrives at the [shop you dislike] warehouse where he finds Becky, playing [card game], inside an old [car model name].

BECKY

MALONE, I KNEW YOU WOULD FIND ME. IF YOU HAD BEEN [your age] MINUTES LATE, I WOULD HAVE BEEN SQUISHED LIKE [takeaway food].

Malone grabs Becky's cards and [action word] them aside.

MALONE

NO TIME TO CHIT-CHAT BECKY, WE'RE NOT SAFE UNTIL WE GET OUT OF THIS [favourite dessert]. WE NEED TO DISGUISE OURSELVES, PUT THIS ON.

Malone hands Becky a [your favourite superhero] outfit. Malone puts on his [best spy gadget]. Just as Malone begins to lift Becky out there is an explosion. Malone and Becky [dance style] left to find better cover.

MALONE

WATCH OUT! THEY'VE PUT [vegetable you hate] EVERYWHERE. STAY CLOSE OR WE'RE FRIED [insect].

BECKY

OH, THAT SOUNDS TASTY. CAN WE GET THAT FOR DINNER TONIGHT BEFORE WE SEE [favourite film]?

MALONE

WHAT DID I SAY ABOUT CHIT-CHAT?

Art Attack

Max Finder
MYSTERY

The Case of the
Art Attack

Did you know that the tongue of a blue whale weighs more than a full-grown elephant? Max Finder here, fact collector and ace detective. Sometimes detectives have to go looking for mysteries. Other times they leap right out in front of you.

My sculpture! It's gone!

That came from Layne Jennings's garden. She sounds angry.

Let's check it out!

Layne is in our class. She loves making art and her back garden is like a messy artist's studio. Tomorrow is the big art competition at school. Layne was going to enter her latest sculpture.

Yesterday, I finished making my newest sculpture and when I checked on it this morning, it was gone! I don't care if I win the competition. I just want to find out who stole it.

Layne's sculpture looked cool. For a month, she'd collected rubbish from the school grounds, then put it all together and created something from nothing.

Don't worry, Layne. We'll find your sculpture and the person who took it.

It's all my dad's fault. He left the gate open yesterday. Anyone could have taken it, but I bet it was Ursula Curtis. She's entering the competition, too.

Ursula is in my art class. She lives nearby. We should pay her a visit.

Uhh...why is that lady staring at us?

That's Janet, my neighbour. She hurt her back rock climbing and is off work. She hates my sculpture. She complains that my hammering keeps her awake.

I added Janet to our suspect list, right below Ursula. Before we rushed off to ask them questions, Alison and I searched Layne's garden for clues.

It looks like the thief dropped a flower, but I can't work out these tracks.

Searching a crime scene can be a tricky job. You never know what clues you'll stumble over or step in.

After we cleaned up Alison's shoe, we went next door to chat with Janet. She just smiled when we told her about the missing sculpture.

Gross! I bet that's from Janet's dog, Rascal. He always gets into our garden.

Making noise with a hammer isn't art! Maybe now Layne will take up painting and we'll all get some peace and quiet around here.

We were on our way to talk to Ursula when we ran into Nicholas Musicco. He was out fishing with his dad. They didn't catch any fish, but they did catch a clue.

Someone dumped a weird metal thing in the river. It's polluting the water!

It's Layne's sculpture! The thief must have dumped it over the bridge.

That's half the case solved. Let's find the loser who did this.

Move it or lose it, detectives!

Watch it, Basher!

WOOSH!

Basher McGintley may be the planet's biggest bully, but even he wouldn't ignore Alison when she's angry. We caught up with him at the bottom of the hill.

Some of Layne's art was taken, Basher. What do you know about it?

I didn't take her dumb sculpture! But I did see Ursula nosing around Layne's back garden after school yesterday.

Basher wouldn't tell us much more. He just wanted to get back into his soapbox racer. On our way to Ursula's house, we made a pit stop to call Layne and tell her about her sculpture.

Layne didn't sound too surprised to hear that we found her sculpture in the river.

Weird.

When we finally got to Ursula's house, she was in her garage working on her entry for the art competition. We told her how we found the stolen sculpture in the river.

Basher says you were hanging around Layne's garden yesterday, Ursula.

You detectives are totally clueless. Layne knew she'd never win against my masterpiece. That's why she dumped her own sculpture in the river! Layne is your thief.

When we left Ursula, I couldn't get what she said out of my head. Was Layne so scared of losing the competition that she faked the whole sculpture theft?

Do you really think Layne is setting us up?

There she is now. Don't let her see us!

That's her dad, helping her get the sculpture out of the river. She doesn't look happy.

With the gate left open, anyone could have taken the sculpture. Or maybe Ursula's right and Layne made it all up and dumped her art into the river!

I think you dumped your brain in the river, Max. I know who stole the sculpture and why.

Do you know who stole the sculpture? All the clues are here. Turn to page 78 for the solution.

What Is It?

Take a shot and see how many of these garage close-ups you can name!

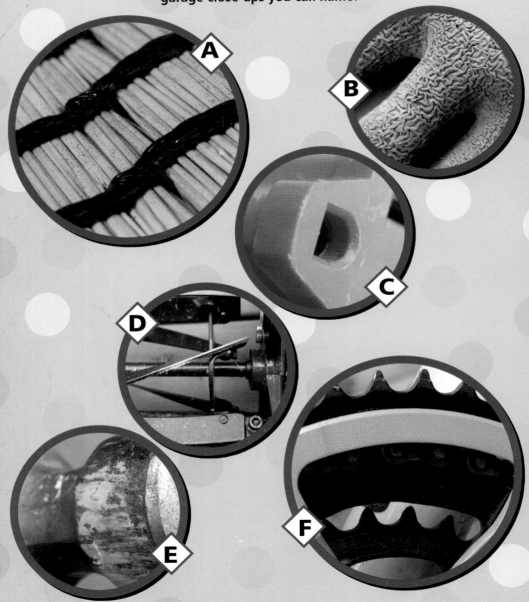

A

B

C

D

E

F

ANSWERS ON PAGE 83

Snake Escape

Max Finder

MYSTERY

The Case of the Snake Escape

Did you know the human brain is 80% water? Max Finder here, fact collector and ace detective. It's early Sunday morning and I should still be in bed, but Alison got a call from our friend Jeff Coleman. And we have a fresh mystery to solve.

Jeff wasn't kidding when he said there was trouble at his dad's pet shop.

He sounded worried on the phone, but I didn't expect the police to be here.

Hey! Watch it, jerk!

Easy, Alison. That's Lukas Hajduk. He squashes kids like us for fun.

The police were there, but they weren't taking Jeff's dad seriously.

A missing snake is not a crime, Mr Coleman! We've got no signs of a break-in. It probably slipped out of the front door when you weren't looking.

But, you don't understand--

When the police left, we went into the pet shop. Jeff filled us in on the details.

Last night, Kong, our biggest king snake, escaped from his tank. We can't find him anywhere and he's hard to miss. He's almost as long as a ping-pong table!

King snake?! Sounds dangerous.

Kong is the one in danger! King snakes are harmless, but need special care. If he slithered out of the shop, he could die. You've got to help us find him.

I told you last week, Annette. My answer is no! Don't ask me again. Now, help us find Kong!

Annette looks pretty ticked off.

Sounds like Dad turned her down for a raise again. No surprise there. It's her fault Kong is missing. She forgot to lock the back door last night!

Why is that air vent cover on upside down? Weird.

GAAAAH!

Hi! Sorry I scared you. Are you Alison? Jeff says you're a detective. Are you really?

The chatterbox was Stefanie. She loved hanging out at the pet shop. Her brother Eric used to work in the jewellery shop next door, but lost his job last week.

Stefanie was here first thing to help look for Kong. We didn't even have to call her!

Sorry I scared you. My brother says I'm great at hiding. Hey, Jeff. Did you tell them about Lukas?

Two days ago, Lukas Hajduk came into the store and wanted to buy Kong. My dad said he wasn't old enough to look after a king snake.

Lukas lost it. He yelled at Mr Coleman and stormed out of the shop!

55

We talked to Annette, the shop manager. She swore that she locked all the doors and double-checked them before leaving. She was the last one to see Kong in his tank.

Both Annette and Lukas were mad at Mr Coleman and had a motive for taking Kong. We had no snake, but we had two suspects. We decided to track down suspect number two.

Lukas always rides his bike at the skate park on weekends.

Stefanie stuck around the shop until we closed. She must have gone out of the front door while I was in the back office doing the paperwork. Then I went home and watched TV.

Let's ask BMX-boy a few questions.

Lukas denied stealing Kong, but he did have some interesting news about Annette. Lukas's older sister was friends with the pet shop manager.

Annette said that if she got turned down for a raise again, she'd quit and make Mr Coleman sorry he ever said no to her.

Lukas told us to get lost, so we went back to the pet shop. They still hadn't found Kong. Stefanie's brother Eric was there and he was in a hurry to leave.

Give me a call when you find Kong!

Stefanie and Eric's dad was in an accident last year and can't work. Eric helps out, but they don't have a lot of money. Without Eric's job, it will be tougher for them.

The next day was Monday. Before school started, we cruised by the pet shop to see if Kong had turned up. He hadn't, but the police had.

The jewellery shop was robbed last night!

Some diamonds were missing and the police were taking this crime seriously. While they were talking to Mr Li, the shop owner, we took a closer look at the crime scene.

I'm the only one with keys to the shop. We were closed yesterday, and I'm sure I turned on the security alarm. I don't know how they got in.

There are no signs of a break-in. The thief knew the alarm code and took the tapes from the security cameras! Looks like an inside job to me.

The diamonds must have been taken on Saturday night. That's when the alarm was turned off.

That means the diamonds and Kong disappeared at the same time!

We don't have time to catch a diamond thief. Kong is still missing!

Don't shed your skin, Jeff. The diamond theft and Kong's escape are connected. I know where Kong is.

And I know who's behind it all.

Do you know who's behind Kong's disappearance? All the clues are here. Turn to page 78 for the answers.

Photo Play

Only three identical pet photos appear in all three boxes below. **Can you find them?**

ANSWER ON PAGE 83

Bicycle Bandit

Max Finder

MYSTERY

The Case of the Bicycle Bandit

Did you know there are more than a billion bicycles in the world? Max Finder here, fact collector and ace detective. It's a sunny Saturday here in Whispering Meadows and we're in the middle of the most boring stakeout in detective history - ever.

My butt is numb, Max.

I've read this magazine a hundred times. The bike thief isn't coming. Can we go?

The kid with the numb butt is Nicholas Musicco, our newest client. Last weekend, some idiot stole his bike from the bike rack while he was swimming in the pool. It's a red BMX with a blue stripe. Not easy to miss, but we have no clues.

There's the Big Scoop van. Who wants ice cream?

Now you're talking!

The Big Scoop ice cream van comes to the pool every Saturday. That is, when the van isn't broken down. Glen sells ice cream for a local ice-cream company.

Sorry I'm late. I had to pick up some fresh coffee from the Free Wheelin' cafe. At least the pool is busier than the skate park. I just spent an hour sitting there doing nothing!

SKREEEEEEEES

Max! Somebody stole my bike! You've gotta help me!

The bicycle bandit strikes again!

We were staking out the wrong spot!

The skate park was pretty quiet for a Saturday. Crystal said she locked up her bike with a really strong lock. They got some ice cream from the Big Scoop van and skated for about an hour.

When I came back to the rack, my bike was gone!

Bike thieves won't let even the toughest locks stop them. Some use hacksaws or hammers to break a lock. Some even use car jacks to pry open locks.

Looks like oil.

Our thief made a mess when he took your bike.

Did you see anyone hanging around the bike racks?

Lance Reeves was here looking for his brother Felix, but that could have been just an excuse.

I've heard of Lance. He's a bicycle courier. He tried to sell my brother some illegal video games last month. Maybe he's selling stolen bikes now.

All the bike couriers in town hang out at the Free Wheelin' Café. Even though it was Saturday, we decided to take a chance and swing by. It paid off. Lance was there, talking to his little brother Felix. Lance didn't sound happy.

You tell Lukas a deal is a deal. I want my money today!

FREE WHEEL Café

Lance and Felix went inside the café and we checked out the alley.

Crystal's bike lock!

It looks like Lance was back here dumping the evidence.

The lock had been pulled apart by something very strong and it was covered in the same oil that we found at the bike racks.

There goes Felix. We can't let him get away!

Felix rode across town like his bike was on fire. We followed him into an unfamiliar neighbourhood. The person he was visiting, however, was very familiar.

That's Lukas Hajduk! I knew that creep was involved.

We need to get a closer look at that garage.

When Felix left, we made our move and found our second piece of evidence.

That's Nicholas's bike! Lukas is the bike thief!

I'm no bike thief. Now get out of here before I let the air out of your heads!

Lukas!

Lukas said his dad bought the bike for his little brother from an auction website. The bike came in the post and they didn't even meet the person selling it. The bike was definitely Nicholas's. But Lukas wouldn't hand it over and I wasn't going to make him.

It's gonna be hard to catch a thief in cyberspace.

On the ride home, we passed the Big Scoop ice cream van. A flat tyre had put it out of business for the day.

Broken down again, Glen?

Yep, but I can fix this old van blindfolded!

Back at my place, Alison and I logged onto the auction website that Lukas told us about. Nicholas's bike was still for sale and that raised more questions.

auctionworld

FOR SALE BMX

contact: boscopig@auctionworld.com

Maybe the thief hasn't removed it from the site yet.

Or Lukas is lying. He could be the one selling the bike over the Internet.

I'm stumped, Max.

contact: boscopig @ auctionworld.com

Me too, but I think this email address will give us some answers.

Do you know who the bike thief is? All the clues are here. Turn to page 79 for the answers.

Suspect Scramble

Every detective needs a list of possible suspects.
Max changed his suspect's names into anagrams.
Can you unscramble the anagrams and uncover the suspects?
Write your answers on a separate piece of paper.

HINT: The suspect list contains four of the following seven people:
Dorothy Pafko, Basher McGintley, Crystal Diallo, Tony DeMatteo,
Josh Spodek, Ethan Webster or Leslie Chang.

JOKED SHOPS

RADICALLY LOST

MASTERY BELCHING

CLEAN SLEIGH

ANSWERS ON PAGE 84

White Pine Werewolf

Max Finder
MYSTERY

The Case of the **White Pine Werewolf**

Did you know you can smell plants better just before a rainstorm? Max Finder here, ace detective and fact collector. It's finally summer. That means two weeks at White Pine Summer Camp — and counsellor John Chu's spooky ghost stories!

Tonight I'll tell you about the curse of the White Pine Werewolf.

More like the curse of the lame summer camp!

A hundred years ago, these woods were filled with loggers and wolves. One moonlit evening, not far from this camp, a mysterious wolf bit a logger called Big Jim.

The wolf bite changed Big Jim. Red fur sprouted on his body and sharp teeth grew in his mouth. Big Jim turned into a werewolf and he was hungry!

Big Jim wandered back to his camp, looking for loggers to eat. When the loggers saw the huge wolf and heard its howls echoing through the trees, they ran into the woods screaming and never returned to the camp.

To this day, the White Pine Werewolf stalks the woods looking for campers who have strayed too far – so beware!

John Chu tells the same old story every year! This camp is for losers.

Jessica and Sasha are just bitter because they didn't get to travel to the USA this summer.

The next day...

TUCK SHOP

Max, someone broke into the camp shop last night!

Inside, the shop was a mess. Carla Baxter, the counsellor in charge of the camp shop, said she locked up at 10:00pm and then went straight to sleep in her cabin.

Some packets of sweets are missing. Do you think badgers dragged them outside?

There are no drag marks near the door.

Badgers don't open bags neatly along the seam, like this one.

And badgers don't have red fur.

Red fur!

It's the White Pine Werewolf!

SOUR CREAM & ONION

Rumours that the White Pine Werewolf had ransacked the shop spread through the camp faster than wildfire.

I'm not going into the woods if that werewolf is out there!

Me neither!

Alison and I knew there was no werewolf. Someone was using the legend to cover their tracks and we were going to catch them.

You were right, John. Now that the camp shop is closed, I can go outside and have fun. I hated being stuck in there.

Irene, the camp cook, wasn't sad to see the shop closed down either.

You kids might start eating the food I cook, now that there are no sweets to ruin your appetites.

After breakfast, Alison went canoeing, and I worked on my mask project. I asked Jessica about the break-in.

I'd love to help with your mystery, Max, but I was tucked away in my bed last night.

Alison took a break from her paddle across the lake and chatted with Leslie Chang.

John said he got all these chocolate bars from Carla. Maybe she robbed the camp shop!

Carla said she was asleep in her cabin while the robbery happened.

Whatever! I'm in Dew Drop cabin. That's Carla's cabin. Last night, she was gone so long that Jessica and Sasha had time to sneak out, too.

On my way to lunch, I met Mr Payton, the camp groundskeeper.

Irene borrowed this garden tool yesterday. Now it's dented and covered in brown paint!

Irene says she left the garden tool exactly as she found it – undamaged and outside the tool shed.

But Mr Payton found it in the bushes behind Dew Drop cabin.

The werewolf is in the cave! *Help!*

The cave wasn't far into the woods, so Alison and I checked it out.

It's pretty dark in there.

There are no wolf prints, but plenty of sweet wrappers.

That night...

The mysterious werewolf has everyone too scared for a ghost story tonight.

There's no mystery. The White Pine Werewolf is sitting at this fire right now.

Do you know who robbed the camp store and is pretending to be the White Pine Werewolf? All the clues are here. Turn to page 80 to find out.

FISHY Warning

Campers at White Pine Summer Camp are being warned not to swim in the lake because it's full of hungry piranhas! Read the clues below to find out if the story is true.
How did you crack the case?

WHITE PINE GAZETTE

No Swimming Allowed

Every summer, White Pine Lake has hundreds of campers visiting it. Even though the water never gets warmer than 19°C (66°F), campers love to swim in it. There are rumours that piranhas have made the lake home. Now no one dares enter the tiny freshwater lake. Everyone misses swimming in the lake, but no one wants to risk being attacked by the piranhas.

If you get stuck, hold these clues up to a mirror.

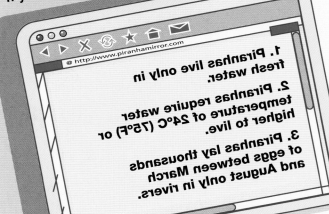

@ http://www.piranhamirror.com

1. Piranhas live only in fresh water.

2. Piranhas require water temperature of 24°C (75°F) or higher to live.

3. Piranhas lay thousands of eggs between March and August only in rivers.

ANSWER ON PAGE 84

Who? What? When? Where? How? Why?

Who? What? When?

The Case of the Basketball Card Foul

(page 11)

Who stole the Vince McGrady basketball card?

- **Josh "Rumbler" Spodek.** During the basketball game, he faked his injury. While he was alone in the boys' changing room, he took the card from Ethan's gym bag because he was tired of listening to Ethan brag about the card.

How did Alison crack the case?

- Alison realised Rumbler's injury was faked when she saw him carrying a big bag filled with Bouncy Bears at the comic and card convention.
- When she saw that Rumbler had a little sister, Alison knew he was the thief. Rumbler got his little sister to ring the Player's Den Card Shop and ask about selling the Vince McGrady card. Rumbler was a regular customer and the shop assistant would recognise his deep voice.

What were the others doing at the card show?

- Coach Sweeny had just bought a rare basketball card to add to his collection.
- Crystal really was looking for a birthday present for her brother.
- Leo Ducharme was so embarrassed to be seen with a Bouncy Bears collection that he ran away from the detectives.

Conclusion

When Max and Alison confronted Rumbler, he confessed to stealing the basketball card. Fortunately for Ethan, Rumbler hadn't sold it yet and he returned it. Although Ethan was mad at his friend for stealing, they eventually made up and continue to work together on and off the basketball court.

The Case of the Midnight Scratcher

(page 17)

Who scratched the CD?

- **Emma Chang.** She was jealous of Leslie's friendship with Gabrielle and wanted to make Leslie so mad at Gabrielle that they would never be friends again. Emma sneaked into the living room and put on Gabrielle's socks. She used the light of the fridge to help her see as she scratched Leslie's CD with her brother Doug's knife.

How did Max solve the case?

- When Max and Alison arrived at Leslie's house, they heard Emma complain about Gabrielle.
- Dorothy Pafko only saw Gabrielle's socks. The fridge door hid the rest of the person in the kitchen. Emma hoped one of the girls would wake up and see the coloured socks and assume it was Gabrielle.

- Dorothy didn't see the person's head because the fridge door was in the way. But Gabrielle is tall. If Gabrielle had been in the kitchen, Dorothy would have seen

How? Why? Where?

Case Solutions

her head poking over the top of the fridge door. Gabrielle's impersonator must have been short, like Emma.

- When Nanda complained about the door leading to the bedrooms opening in the middle of the night, Max knew it was Emma sneaking from her bedroom into the living room.

Conclusion

When Emma was confronted with the facts, she apologised and agreed to buy Leslie a new CD. Now Leslie and Gabrielle let Emma play hula hoops with them, and she's getting pretty good.

The Case of the Stereo-Smashing Spook

(page 23)

Who smashed Tony's stereo?

- **Nanda Kanwar.** Mad at Tony for winning the costume contest, Nanda decided to hide the stereo and give him a scare. But her Halloween trick went wrong.
- Nanda pretended to be Leslie Chang by putting on her costume. Leslie was running the dance and no one would stop her from taking the stereo from the gym.
- Nanda planned to hide the stereo behind the ticket table but, as she was moving the table out of the way, the trolley rolled forward, sending the stereo smashing down the stairs.

How did Max solve the case?

- There was green face paint on Leslie's cloak. Nanda's green face paint had wiped off around her neck from wearing the cloak.
- Both Tony and Leo said the person who took the stereo had big green feet. Nanda's costume had big green feet.
- Nanda lied about seeing Leslie wheel the trolley out of the gym to clear her name. Nanda was the one pushing the trolley!
- Max and Alison didn't tell anyone where Basher was hiding, but Nanda joked with Dorothy that the bully was hiding under the stairs. Nanda knew because Basher had scared her as she ran away from the smashed stereo.

Conclusion

Nanda confessed to smashing the stereo. It was an accident and she apologised to Tony. She also said sorry to Leslie for trying to put the blame on her. Tony's father fixed the stereo and Tony donated it to the school. Now all the kids use it during rainy day lunchtimes.

75

Who? What? When?

The Case of the Soapy Switch

(page 29)

Who switched the chocolate bars?
• Tony DeMatteo. He switched Nanda's chocolate bars because Alex Rodriguez promised to give him the snowboard.

How did Max and Alison solve the case?
• Max recognised Alex's handwriting on the note. It was the same writing as on the "Chocolates for Charity" sign outside the supermarket.
• Alison knew the script Nanda found belonged to Tony because it had no markings. Tony didn't write on his script because he had no lines in the play.
• The soap shop didn't sell that kind of soap any more, so the culprit must have taken the soap from the storeroom at the shop. The van in Tony's driveway had the same soap shop's logo on it, and Tony's mum was the shop owner. Tony had access to the storeroom and took the soap.

How did Tony make the switch?
• On the bus home, Alex distracted Nanda by rehearsing for the play. Tony sneaked up from behind and switched the chocolate boxes. Tony tried several times before getting it right. That's why the bus driver kept telling him to sit down.

Conclusion
• When confronted with these facts, Alex and Tony admitted to working together to switch the chocolates. Alex was disqualified and Tony returned the stolen chocolate bars.
• Lots of money was raised for charity and Nanda won the snowboard. She was last seen waxing it up and waiting for the first big snowfall of the year.

The Case of the Sandy Ski Hill

(page 35)

Who is the sand dumper?
• **Nate Yamada.** He was so mad at being turned down for the job of ski patroller that he wanted to make the other patrollers look bad.

How did Max solve the case?
• Nate wasn't a real ski patroller. He didn't have a full ski patrol uniform like Carla — he was missing the red ski patrol hat and proper jacket. Carla called him the chairlift operator, which was his real job.
• When Carla told Max about the missing ski patrol vest, Max remembered seeing Nate wearing one and knew Nate was pretending to be a ski patroller.
• The prints in the woods were made by a ski boot. Nanda rides a snowboard, which requires a different type of boot.

Case Solutions

requires a different type of boot.
- The green backpack at the sand bin was Nate's. He was carrying it when he stopped the detectives.

Conclusion
- He stole a ski patrol vest and used his backpack to dump sand on the ski runs. While filling up at the sand bin, Nate was startled by Mr Zilkowsky. He dropped his backpack and fled. Mr Zilkowsky was stealing sand from the bin to put on his path.
- Nate apologised to the ski patrollers and repaired the ski runs. With another snowfall, they'll be back in shape and ready for more shredding.

The Case of the Missing Movie

(page 41)

Who stole the *Dogtown Malone* movie reels?
- **Mrs Doyle.** She didn't want the kids to see *Dogtown Malone* because she felt it was too violent. So she sabotaged the popcorn maker, stole the movie reels, and hid them under the front stage inside the cinema.

How did Max and Alison solve the case?
- Mrs Doyle said she was in Trina's office emptying the rubbish bin when the popcorn maker went haywire. But the bin in the office was still full of rubbish.
- Melanie saw Mrs Doyle picking up rubbish at the front of the cinema. But the floor was covered with litter and the label to the movie reels was there. Mrs Doyle wasn't picking up litter. She was hiding the movie reels under the stage.
- When Mrs Doyle complained about *Dogtown Malone* being too scary for kids, the rubbish bag in her hand was empty.

What were Rumbler, Ethan and Melanie up to?
- Rumbler was helping Ethan sneak into the cinema without paying. Melanie saw them and agreed not to tell anyone if the boys voted to see *Finding Tutu* for next week's movie.

Conclusion
- Mrs Doyle confessed to stealing the reels when Max and Alison found them under the front stage. She was Trina's best usher so she didn't lose her job. Trina even let her wear earplugs during *Dogtown Malone*!

Who? What? When?

The Case of the Art Attack

(page 47)

Who stole Layne's sculpture?
- **Basher McGintley.** Basher saw Ursula nosing around Layne's back garden and she showed him the sculpture. He wanted the wheels for his soapbox racer.
- Basher rode his bike into the garden and loaded the sculpture into his trailer. After he and his friends took the wheels off, they dumped the sculpture into the river.

How did Alison solve the case?
- The bike tracks in the mud by Layne's gate matched Basher's bike and the trailer that carried his soapbox racer tools.
- Alison only told Basher that "Layne's art" was stolen. But Basher knew she meant a sculpture.
- When Layne and her dad loaded the sculpture onto his truck, the detectives noticed the wheels were missing. Alison realised Basher had the wheels on his new soapbox racer!

Conclusion
- After Layne threatened to throw Basher's soapbox racer into the river, the bully confessed to stealing the sculpture. Basher returned the wheels, but not before his dad banned him from riding the racer for a month.
- Ursula apologised for lying to the detectives. She said she couldn't resist giving them the runaround.
- Layne put the wheels back on her sculpture and entered it into the competition. All the judges were impressed with the way she got it to smell like the bottom of a river!

The Case of the Snake Escape

(page 53)

Who is behind Kong's disappearance and the diamond robbery?
- **Stefanie and her brother Eric.** They thought selling the diamonds would solve their money problems.
- Stefanie never left the pet shop on Saturday night. She hid behind Kong's tank and waited until Annette left. Then she let her brother in through the back door.
- Eric crawled through the air vent to the jewellery shop. He used to work in the shop so he knew how to turn off the alarm. He took the tapes from the security cameras, stole the diamonds and then crawled back through the vent.
- They went out of the pet shop's back door, but couldn't lock it. Annette got blamed for leaving it unlocked.

Where is Kong?
- Kong is in the jewellery shop.

How did Kong escape?
- Eric kicked loose the lid to Kong's tank when he was climbing into the air vent. Stefanie was keeping watch out of the front window and didn't see Kong slither

Case Solutions

up the tree and into the air vent into the jewellery shop.

How did Max and Alison solve the case?
- Annette was too busy in the back office doing paperwork to see if Stefanie left the pet store.
- Stefanie came to look for Kong, but nobody had told her he was missing.
- Eric's jacket was torn and it matched the material caught on the air vent in the jewellery shop.

Conclusion
- Stefanie and Eric confessed to taking the diamonds. Kong was found hiding in the jewellery shop.
- Stefanie and Eric got in a lot of trouble and vowed never to steal again. Mr Li didn't want Eric to go to prison, so he forgave Eric and even helped him to find another job.

The Case of the Bicycle Bandit
(page 59)

Who stole the bikes?
- **Glen.** He parked the ice cream van in front of the bike racks. When no one was looking, Glen snapped Crystal's bike lock with a strong car jack. Then he hid the bike in the van and drove off. He did the same to Nicholas's bike at the pool the weekend before.

How did Max and Alison solve the case?
- The oil on Glen's apron matched the oil found near the bike racks and on the broken lock.
- In the rubbish bin there were empty "Big Scoop ice cream" boxes. Glen threw the bike lock and the cartons in the bin when he picked up coffee from the cafe before arriving at the pool.
- Glen complained that he was practically alone at the skate park — that gave him plenty of time to steal a bike.
- The thief was using a leaky car jack to break the locks, just like the one Glen used to change the tyre on the ice-cream van.
- The email address from the auction site was boscopig@auctionworld.com. BOSCOPIG is an anagram for "Big Scoop," the name of the ice-cream company Glen worked for.

Conclusion
- Glen lost his job with the ice-cream company and was sentenced to community service picking up litter at the skate park. He returned Crystal's bike and paid back the money Lukas's dad spent buying Nicholas's bike.
- Lukas owed Lance money for some computer software that he bought. Felix went to Lukas's house to collect the money.
- Nicholas got his bike back and now he uses two locks to secure his bike at the pool.

Who? What? When?

The Case of the White Pine Werewolf

(page 65)

Who robbed the camp shop and pretended to be the White Pine Werewolf?

- **Jessica, with the help of her friend, Sasha.** Jessica had been at White Pine camp last summer, so she knew the legend of the White Pine Werewolf and used it to scare the other campers.

How did Max and Alison solve the case?

- Max saw that Jessica was using red fur to make her mask at the crafts table. It was the same kind of fur found stuck to the door of the camp shop.
- Jessica's mask was inside the cave where the werewolf was spotted. She dropped it after scaring the campers.
- Jessica claimed she was sleeping during the robbery, but Leslie Chang saw Jessica and Sasha leave the cabin that night.
- Mr Payton's gardening tool was dented and covered with paint because they used it to make the scratch marks on the camp shop wall. The tool was found behind Dew Drop cabin – Jessica's cabin – because she threw it there after robbing the shop.

Conclusion

- Since the shop was closed for a clean-up, Carla gave John Chu a bag of chocolate bars to give out to campers during the canoeing trip.
- At the campfire, Max presented these facts to Jessica and Sasha. They confessed to wrecking the camp shop and pretending to be the White Pine werewolf. They were sent home for the summer and had to pay for all the stolen snacks.

Card Caper (page 16)

Jerome Smith is the fake card. The silver hologram should be gold, his team's name is misspelled once and his statistic total is not correct.

His card should read:

YR	TEAM	GP	FG%	FT%	REB	AST	STL	BLK	PTS	AVG
04-05	Volcanoes	69	.428	.731	387	137	75	17	673	8.7
05-06	Volcanoes	75	.475	.740	405	198	71	25	728	8.9
TOTAL		144	.452	.736	792	335	146	42	1401	8.8

Crime Scene Team (page 22)

Dorothy told Max and Alison that she saw the suspect with coloured socks at the fridge. The purple footprints (belonging to the person wearing the coloured socks) went from Emma's bedroom, into the hallway, into the kitchen and to the fridge. Emma Chang scratched the CD. Now turn to page 74 for the full solution.

Message Mix-up (page 28)

The correct order is: h, c, b, d, g, f, i, a and e.
Crystal was mixed-up and wore a witch costume like Leslie. Crystal didn't read through all the instant messages when she returned from shopping. Crystal thought Leslie was going as Frankenstein.

Locker Stalker (page 34)

Tennis. There is a tennis racket and balls.
Trainers: Red (with white and yellow).
Barbecue. Tony has three bags of BBQ crisps.
Yellow. The report is in his binder.
Books: *Kung Fu: For Beginners, Canadian Ornithology, A Guide to Strigiformes, The Big Book of Owls,* or *The Li'l Book of Owls.*
Tennis balls: There are two tennis balls in his locker.
Canada: There is a Canadian flag on his rucksack and a Maid of the Mist snow globe.

Spy Quiz (page 40)

1. **False.** Spying is best used as a way to collect information about a suspect. This information might later help catch or provide proof that a suspect committed a crime.

2. **False.** Spies do use their instincts, but they need to collect as much evidence as possible to help solve a case.

3. **True.** It's best to spy with a team so that you can watch suspects from different angles and places.

4. **False.** Spies hide tiny hidden cameras in watches, coat buttons, sunglasses, baseball caps and bags.

5. **True.** Spies always want to blend into the place they are spying. Camouflage is any clothing that helps do this.

6. **True.** When watching a suspect, a spy should never move his or her head — just his or her eyes. This way the suspect will never know he or she is being watched.

7. **False.** Spies keep notes, take photographs and shoot videos to record what they see.

8. **False.** When a spy is being followed they should continue to walk at normal speed, but make abrupt turns left and right until they are no longer followed.

9. **True.** The spy tries to find the suspect again by tracking footprints.

10. **False.** Both male and female spies may need to disguise themselves as men or women of different ages and ethnicities. Spies need lots of clothes for all occasions plus glasses, wigs and hats.

What Is It? (page 52)

A. Broom
B. Gardening glove
C. Electrical plug
D. Lawn mower blades
E. Hammer
F. Bicycle sprocket

Photo Play (page 58)

The three pets that appear in all three boxes are:

Suspect Scramble (page 64)

The suspects are:

Josh Spodek (joked shops), **Crystal Diallo** (radically lost), **Basher McGintley** (mastery belching), and **Leslie Chang** (clean sleigh).

Tony DeMatteo, Ethan Webster and **Dorothy Pafko** were not on the suspect list.

Fishy Warning (page 72)

It is just a hoax: there are no piranhas in the lake. The lake is too cold for piranhas to live in. Even if the piranhas could survive, they would be unable to lay eggs in the lake. To read the three clues, hold the puzzle up to a mirror. **Clue # 1** says that piranhas require fresh water to live. **Clue # 2** says that piranhas need to live in water 24°C (75°F) or higher. **Clue # 3** says that piranhas only lay eggs in rivers between March and August.

Locker Stalker

(page 34)

Test your memory by trying to answer the following questions:

? What sport does Tony play (other than hockey)?

? What colour are the trainers in Tony's locker?

? What is Tony's favourite flavour of crisps?

? What colour of paper is Tony's report printed on?

? Name two books found in Tony's locker.

? How many balls does Tony have in his locker?

? Where has Tony travelled to recently?

Max has a nose for mysteries and a brain for unusual facts. Like his hero, Sherlock Holmes, Max uses logic and observation to solve mysteries in his home town, Whispering Meadows. When Max isn't solving crimes with Alison, he can be found riding his skateboard, playing on his games console, reading or avoiding Basher McGintley.

Alison Santos

Friends since pre-school, Alison and Max share a passion for mysteries. An aspiring journalist, Alison has an insatiable taste for adventure and desire to uncover the truth. Max and Alison are a real team, as she likes to remind Max: "If it wasn't for me, you'd still be finding lost marbles for the kids in pre-school."

Leslie Chang

Leslie is the ultimate high achiever, a dedicated organiser, and tireless busybody with a juicy piece of gossip on every pupil and teacher at school. She's a great source of information for Max and Alison, except when she is a suspect herself.

Ursula Curtis

A competitive artist, Ursula often paints in bright colours. If she is not painting flowers, she is usually wearing them on her clothes.

Tony DeMatteo

Tony is an all-round athlete. He plays football and is the captain of the hockey team. This sports freak also has a sensitive side and cries at sad movies!

Crystal Diallo

Crystal is a huge comics and manga fan. She loves dressing up, especially as her hero Storm from the X-Men.

Lukas Hajduk

Lukas's baggy jeans and cap are a perfect fit for his BMX bike. Thick-necked and thick-skulled, 14-year-old Lukas was expelled from Central Meadows School and now attends Twindale School.

Nanda Kanwar

Nanda always has the latest music and clothes. This 12-year-old hockey goalkeeper would not hesitate to pass the blame onto a friend if it kept her out of trouble.

Ben "Basher" McGintley

With fists the size of pumpkins, 14-year-old Basher is always looking for fresh stomachs to punch. Basher's scowls and grunts often hide key clues for Max and Alison.

Nicholas Musicco

Nicholas is small for his age and not very athletic. He's confident, well-spoken and possesses a very sharp mind.

Dorothy Pafko

Nicknamed "Dot" by her father, the school site manager, Dorothy is a science whiz.

Josh "Rumbler" Spodek

Known simply as "Rumbler" because of his deep voice, Josh loves fishing and sports. He is often found hanging out with his close friend, Ethan Webster.

Alex Rodriguez

Alex strives to be number one at everything. Aged 12, he hopes to be a millionaire within the next ten years. He's always dressed for success.

Ethan Webster

Captain of the baseball and basketball teams, Ethan is Central Meadows School's star athlete, and his ego and clothing prove it. His bragging often gets him into trouble, but his quick thinking has helped Max and Alison solve cases.

Liam O'Donnell

Liam O'Donnell is the author of many children's books and the creator of *Max Finder Mystery* and the *Graphic Guide Adventures* series of graphic novels. In addition to writing for children, Liam is a teacher, plays video games and goes camping (but not all at the same time). He lives in Toronto, Canada. You can visit him online at: **www.liamodonnell.com.**

Michael Cho

Michael Cho was born in Seoul, South Korea and moved to Canada when he was six years old. A graduate of the Ontario College of Art and Design, his distinctive drawings and comics have appeared in publications across North America. He is currently devoting his time to painting book covers, working on an art book of urban landscapes and creating more comics. You can always see his latest work online at: **www.michaelcho.com**.